**Blastoff! Readers** are carefully developed by literacy experts to build reading stamina and move students toward fluency by combining standards-based content with developmentally appropriate text.

**Level 1** provides the most support through repetition of high-frequency words, light text, predictable sentence patterns, and strong visual support.

**Level 2** offers early readers a bit more challenge through varied sentences, increased text load, and text-supportive special features.

**Level 3** advances early-fluent readers toward fluency through increased text load, less reliance on photos, advancing concepts, longer sentences, and more complex special features.

★ **Blastoff! Universe**

Reading Level

Grade K

Grades 1–3

Grade 4

This edition first published in 2024 by Bellwether Media, Inc.

No part of this publication may be reproduced in whole or in part without written permission of the publisher. For information regarding permission, write to Bellwether Media, Inc., Attention: Permissions Department, 6012 Blue Circle Drive, Minnetonka, MN 55343.

Library of Congress Cataloging-in-Publication Data

Names: Barnes, Rachael, author.
Title: Great horned owls / by Rachael Barnes.
Description: Minneapolis, MN : Bellwether Media, Inc., 2024. | Series: Blastoff! Readers. Who's hoo? Owls! | Includes bibliographical references and index. | Audience: Ages 5-8 | Audience: Grades 2-3 | Summary: "Relevant images match informative text in this introduction to great horned owls. Intended for students in kindergarten through third grade"-- Provided by publisher.
Identifiers: LCCN 2023008911 (print) | LCCN 2023008912 (ebook) | ISBN 9798886874167 (library binding) | ISBN 9798886876048 (ebook)
Subjects: LCSH: Great horned owl--Juvenile literature.
Classification: LCC QL696.S83 B372 2024 (print) | LCC QL696.S83 (ebook) | DDC 598.9/7--dc23/eng/20230323
LC record available at https://lccn.loc.gov/2023008911
LC ebook record available at https://lccn.loc.gov/2023008912

Text copyright © 2024 by Bellwether Media, Inc. BLASTOFF! READERS and associated logos are trademarks and/or registered trademarks of Bellwether Media, Inc.

Editor: Rebecca Sabelko   Designer: Brittany McIntosh

Printed in the United States of America, North Mankato, MN.

# Table of Contents

| | |
|---|---|
| Well-known Hoot! | 4 |
| Diving from Above | 12 |
| Call It Home | 18 |
| Glossary | 22 |
| To Learn More | 23 |
| Index | 24 |

# Well-known Hoot!

ear tuft

Great horned owls are named for their **ear tufts**. They look like horns!

These owls are known for their hoots. They can be heard in North and South America.

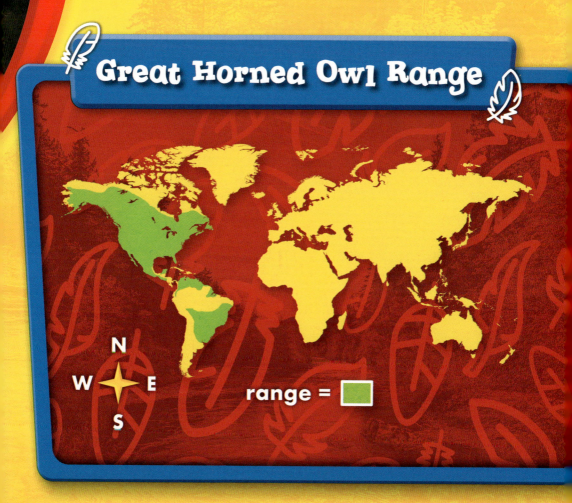

Great Horned Owl Range

range =

Great horned owls are big! They stand about 24 inches (61 centimeters) tall.

Their **wingspan** can reach over 4 feet (1.2 meters) wide.

Great Horned Owl Wingspan

0   1 foot   2 feet   3 feet   4 feet

over 4 feet (1.2 meters) wide

facial disk

Great horned owls have round heads. Their **facial disks** direct sound to their ears.

They have short, **curved** beaks and bright yellow eyes.

Spot a Great Horned Owl!

bright yellow eyes

ear tufts

short, curved beak

Most great horned owls have a mix of gray and brown feathers.

They have white feathers on their necks.

# Diving from Above

perch

Great horned owls often hunt from high **perches** at night.

These owls have excellent eyesight and hearing. They easily find **prey** in the dark!

prey

Once they spot prey, these owls dive silently toward their meal.

They catch birds and small **mammals** with their sharp **talons**!

talons

## Great Horned Owl Food

birds

small mammals

Adult great horned owls are safe from most **predators**.

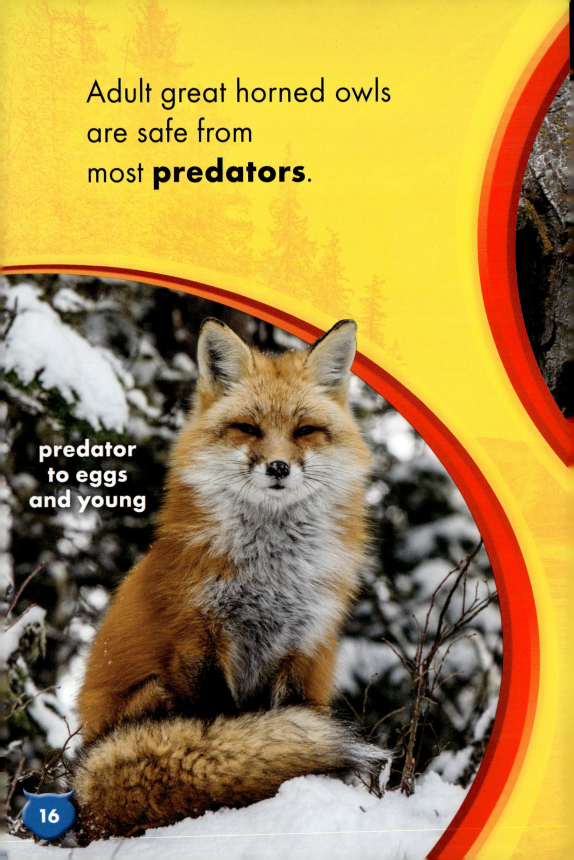

predator to eggs and young

But their eggs and young are prey to crows and foxes.

# Call It Home

roosting in a tree

Great horned owls often call forests home. But they can live in many places.

They **roost** in trees, on cliffs, and in some buildings.

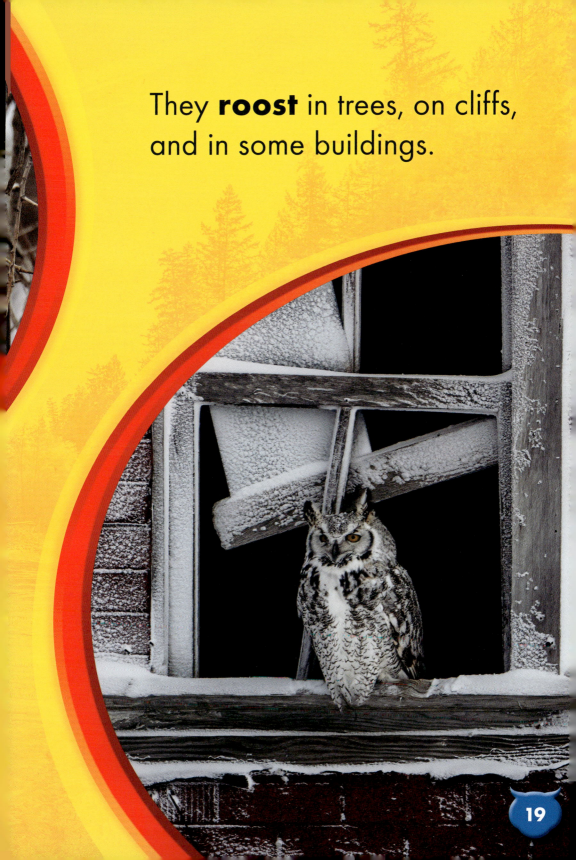

Females usually lay two to three eggs. Soon fluffy **owlets** are born.

**Fledglings** grow adult feathers. They learn to fly. They are ready to live on their own!

fledgling

# Glossary

**curved**—having a hook

**ear tufts**—feathers on the heads of great horned owls; ear tufts are not used for hearing.

**facial disks**—the feathers that cover owls' faces

**fledglings**—young owls that have feathers for flight

**mammals**—warm-blooded animals that have backbones and feed their young milk

**owlets**—baby owls

**perches**—places to sit or rest above the ground

**predators**—animals that hunt other animals for food

**prey**—animals that are hunted by other animals for food

**roost**—to rest in a high place

**talons**—the strong, sharp claws of owls and other raptors

**wingspan**—the distance from the tip of one wing to the tip of the other wing

## To Learn More

### AT THE LIBRARY

Neuenfeldt, Elizabeth. *Barn Owls*. Minneapolis, Minn.: Bellwether Media, 2024.

Taylor, Charlotte. *Great Horned Owls: Striking from Above*. New York, N.Y.: Enslow Publishing, 2022.

Whipple, Annette. *Whooo Knew? The Truth About Owls*. New York, N.Y.: Reycraft Books, 2020.

### ON THE WEB

Factsurfer.com gives you a safe, fun way to find more information.

1. Go to www.factsurfer.com.

2. Enter "great horned owls" into the search box and click 🔍.

3. Select your book cover to see a list of related content.

# Index

adults, 16, 20
beaks, 9
colors, 9, 10, 11
dive, 14
ear tufts, 4, 9
eggs, 16, 17, 20
eyes, 9
eyesight, 13
facial disks, 8
feathers, 10, 11, 20
females, 20
fledglings, 20
fly, 20
food, 14, 15
forests, 18
growing up, 21
heads, 8
hearing, 13
hoots, 5
hunt, 12

name, 4
necks, 11
night, 12
North America, 5
owlets, 20, 21
perches, 12
predators, 16, 17
prey, 13, 14, 17
range, 5
roost, 18, 19
safe, 16
size, 6, 7, 9
South America, 5
talons, 14
wingspan, 7
young, 16, 17

The images in this book are reproduced through the courtesy of: DnDavis, front cover, pp. 6, 10; JayPierstorff, p. 3; All Canada Photos/ Alamy, p. 4; Rob Palmer Photography, p. 7; jadimages, p. 8; kojihirano, p. 9; pchoui, p. 11; TheodoreEmery, p. 12; E.R. Degginger/ Alamy, p. 13; Touched by light images, pp. 14, 21 (top right); wonderful-Earth.net/ Alamy, pp. 14-15; Krumpelman Photography, p. 15 (top left); Jim Cumming, p. 15 (top right); Paul J Hartley, p. 16; Ronnie Howard, p. 17; Mc Photo/ Alamy, p. 18; Pictureguy, p. 19; Ray Hennessy, p. 20; Agnieszka Bacal, pp. 20-21; Stan Tekiela Author/ Naturalist/ Wildlife Photography/ Getty Images, p. 21 (top left); TPCImagery - Mike Jackson, p. 21 (top middle); Chase D'animulls, p. 23.